Published by Creative Education
P.O. Box 227, Mankato, Minnesota 56002
Creative Education is an imprint of The Creative Company

Design and production by Blue Design
Printed in the United States of America

Photographs by Corbis (Bettmann), Getty Images (Jonathan Daniel, Louis DeLuca/MLB Photos, Diamond
Images, Jerry Driendl, Focus on Sport, Bob Gomel//Time Life Pictures, Brad Mangin/MLB Photos, TED
MATHIAS/AFP, Ronald C. Modra/Sports Imagery, Doug Pensinger/Allsport, Hy Peskin/Time Life Pictures,
Photofile/MLB Photos, Rich Pilling/MLB Photos, Herb Scharfman/Sports Imagery, Ezra Shaw, Jamie Squire,
Perry Thorsvik, Tony Tomsic/MLB Photos, Hank Walker//Time Life Pictures, Nick Wass)

Library of Congress Cataloging-in-Publication Data

Omoth, Tyler.
The story of the Baltimore Orioles / by Tyler Omoth.
p. cm. — (Baseball: the great American game)
Includes index.
ISBN-13: 978-1-58341-480-4
1. Baltimore Orioles (Baseball team)—History—Juvenile literature. I. Title. II. Series.

GV875.B2O66 2007
796.357'64097526—dc22   2006029812

First Edition
9 8 7 6 5 4 3 2 1

Cover: Shortstop Miguel Tejada
Page 1: Outfielder Frank Robinson
Page 3: Second baseman Brian Roberts

THE STORY OF THE

BALTIMORE
ORIOLES

by Tyler Omoth

CAL RIPKEN JR.

THE STORY OF THE
Baltimore Orioles

 t was a packed house at Oriole Park at Camden Yards on September 6, 1995. Fans had gathered to celebrate a feat 13 years in the making. After a strike-shortened season in 1994, many fans were upset by the greed and selfishness that seemed to have taken over their national pastime. But on this night, an honest and dependable hero broke an unbreakable record. Cal Ripken Jr. played in his 2,131st consecutive game, breaking a mark previously held by New York Yankees legend Lou Gehrig. As the game between the Baltimore Orioles and the California Angels became official at the end of the fifth inning, play was stopped to acknowledge Ripken's feat, and the longtime shortstop jogged a lap around the stadium, shaking hands and thanking the faithful who had cheered him on. Ripken's humility and sincerity marked the beginning of baseball's comeback into the hearts and minds of the American public.

BROWNS COME TO BALTIMORE

altimore, Maryland, is one of America's oldest and most culturally rich communities. Located on scenic Chesapeake Bay on the East Coast, Baltimore hosts such historic sites as Fort McHenry, whose defense against the British in the War of 1812 inspired Francis Scott Key to write the words to "The Star Spangled Banner," America's national anthem. Baltimore has also featured more than its share of famous citizens, including author Edgar Allan Poe and baseball great George Herman "Babe" Ruth.

Although Ruth never played for Baltimore, the city has a rich tradition in the game—a tradition with roots in St. Louis, Missouri, and a team called the Browns. The St. Louis Browns began playing in the American League (AL) in 1902, and they took their lumps. In their 52-year history, the Browns finished dead last in the AL 14 times and second-to-last in 12 other seasons.

Despite their consistently poor records, the Browns did feature some great players, including Hall of Fame first baseman George Sisler, steady pitcher Urban Shocker, and slugging left fielder Ken Williams, all of whom starred in the 1920s. The Browns finally broke into the postseason in 1944,

Arriving in 1954, the Orioles became Baltimore's second major pro sports team, joining football's Colts.

BALTIMORE

GENE WOODLING

when All-Star shortstop Vern Stephens led St. Louis to the AL pennant with an 89–65 record. The Browns could not complete the heartwarming story, though, losing the World Series to the crosstown St. Louis Cardinals four games to two.

After that World Series defeat, the Browns went back to their losing ways for a decade. In 1951, new Browns owner Bill Veeck struggled to keep the team's popularity up in a city that was home to the more successful Cardinals. He hoped to run the Cards out of town and even went as far as decorating the stadium that the two teams shared, Sportsman's Park, entirely in Browns paraphernalia. When the Anheuser Busch beer company purchased the Cardinals, however, Veeck knew that they were there for good and that his Browns were the odd ones out.

It was then, before the 1954 season, that Veeck sold the franchise to a group of Baltimore businessmen, who quickly relocated the club and renamed it the Baltimore Orioles after the Maryland state bird. The first Orioles team of 1955 fared no better than its Browns predecessors had, finishing seventh in the eight-team AL. Despite the efforts of Stephens and such players as power-hitting catcher Gus Triandos and slick-fielding outfielder Gene Woodling, things did not improve much throughout the 1950s. Still, Baltimore fans filled the stands of Memorial Stadium game after game in support of their new team, providing a foundation on which the franchise would build.

PITCHER · JIM PALMER

Known for his high-kick delivery, Jim Palmer played his entire big-league career in an Orioles uniform and holds club records for strikeouts, wins, shutouts, and complete games. Over his 19-year career, he also assembled a remarkable 2.86 ERA. In 1966, his first season as a regular in the Orioles' rotation, he became the youngest pitcher ever (just under 21 years of age) to hurl a complete-game shutout in the World Series. After missing the entire 1968 season with an arm injury, he went on to become a 20-game winner in 8 seasons and to capture the Cy Young Award 3 times (1973, 1975, and 1976).

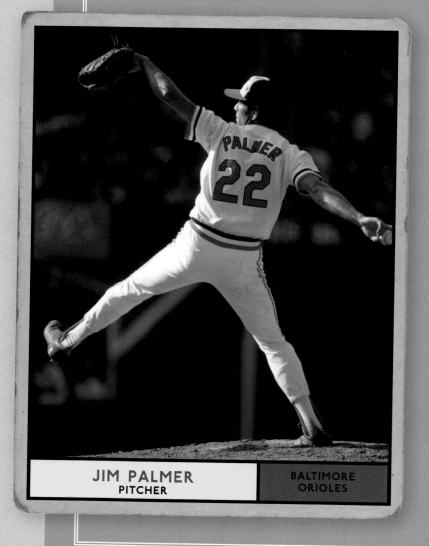

JIM PALMER
PITCHER

BALTIMORE
ORIOLES

STATS

Orioles seasons: 1965–67, 1969–84

Height: 6-3

Weight: 196

- 268–152 career record

- 2,212 career strikeouts

- 6-time All-Star

- Baseball Hall of Fame inductee (1990)

LITTLE EDDIE AT THE BAT

St. Louis Browns owner Bill Veeck was notorious for the publicity stunts he used to put fans in the seats. He once promoted "Grandstand Manager's Day," during which fans in attendance were given "Yes/No" cards and allowed to make all team decisions regarding such moves as stealing bases, bunting, and changing pitchers (the Browns won the game 5–3). But perhaps Veeck's most outrageous stunt came during the second game of a 1951 double-header against the Detroit Tigers. In the bottom of the first inning, Browns manager Zack Taylor sent newly signed Eddie Gaedel up to the plate as a pinch hitter. What made the substitution notable was that Gaedel was a dwarf who stood only 3-foot-7! Once the diminutive hitter's contract had been presented, the umpire allowed Gaedel, who wore jersey number 1/8, to bat. Tigers pitcher Bob Cain was laughing as he prepared to pitch to the tiniest strike zone in major-league history. Not surprisingly, Gaedel walked on four pitches and was then promptly taken out of the game for a pinch runner. Although AL president Will Harridge would void Gaedel's contract the next day, the St. Louis crowd loved the stunt, giving the small batsman a standing ovation as he left the field.

THE ROBINSONS

 ith the money made from its robust fan attendance, the team began to invest heavily in its minor-league system. Baltimore's plan was to develop young players by instilling a philosophy of solid fundamentals and professional attitude. The plan came to be known as the "Oriole Way," a principle the team follows to this day. "There are no shortcuts to where we want to go," said Baltimore manager Paul Richards. "We plan to build this team from the ground up."

The first great player produced by the Oriole Way was a gangly third baseman named Brooks Robinson. Brought to the majors for the first time as an 18-year-old in 1955, Robinson's weak bat kept him going back and forth between the Orioles and the minors for five years. Finally, Baltimore pitchers begged the team to keep Robinson with the big-league club because of his remarkable defense. In 1960, Robinson stayed, and both he and the team had a breakthrough year. Led by rookie pitcher Chuck Estrada's league-leading 18 victories, shortstop Ron Hansen's 22 homers, and Robinson's .294 batting average and Gold Glove-winning play at third base, the Orioles posted their first winning season at 89–65.

RON HANSEN — The 6-foot-3 and 200-pound Hansen was one of the game's biggest shortstops yet was known for his smooth fielding style. He earned All-Star and AL Rookie of the Year honors in 1960, but back problems later hampered his career.

Over the course of 23 seasons with Baltimore, Brooks Robinson earned the nickname "The Human Vacuum Cleaner."

BROOKS ROBINSON

CATCHER · CHRIS HOILES

Catchers love to have a reputation as selfless players who aren't afraid to do the dirty work to help their team win. Chris Hoiles had such a reputation. Hoiles was never an All-Star, nor did he ever win a Gold Glove award for his defense. What he brought to the team was a bit of power at the plate and a knack for getting on base. Hoiles's best season was 1993, when he hit .310 while blasting 29 home runs and driving in 82 runs. Over the course of a 10-year career with the Orioles, the fan favorite was also solid, if not spectacular, behind the plate.

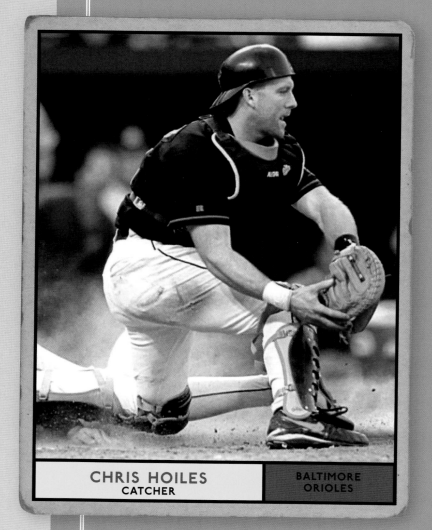

CHRIS HOILES
CATCHER

BALTIMORE
ORIOLES

STATS

Orioles seasons: 1989–98

Height: 6-0

Weight: 213

- .262 career BA
- .994 career fielding percentage
- 151 career HR
- 122 career doubles

The Orioles remained a contender through the mid-1960s, but despite winning 90 or more games 4 times, they could not capture the pennant. Searching for the missing ingredient that would put the team over the top, Baltimore traded pitcher Milt Pappas and two other players to the Cincinnati Reds for outfielder Frank Robinson in 1965. The 30-year-old Robinson had won the 1961 National League Most Valuable Player (MVP) award, but Reds management decided that he was past his prime and traded him. It was a move Cincinnati would regret.

In 1966, Frank Robinson led the AL with a .316 average, 49 home runs, and 122 runs batted in (RBI), capturing the Triple Crown (leading the league in all three categories). Meanwhile, Brooks Robinson added 23 home runs and 100 RBI, and young hurlers Jim Palmer and Dave McNally anchored a talented pitching staff. Behind these efforts, the Orioles soared to a pennant-winning 97–63 record.

In the World Series, Baltimore faced the Los Angeles Dodgers, who featured two of the most feared pitchers in the game: Don Drysdale and Sandy Koufax. In Game 1, both Robinsons slugged home runs in a 5–2 Orioles victory. The favored Dodgers never recovered, and Baltimore rolled to a four-game sweep and its first world championship. "To do that to a ballclub as good as the Dodgers is almost unthinkable," exclaimed Brooks Robinson. "I'm just glad I was here to see it."

THE ORIOLE WAY

altimore was unable to maintain its championship ways, declining in the two years that followed. Midway through the 1968 season, manager Hank Bauer was fired and replaced by Earl Weaver. The fiery new skipper had previously managed the organization's top minor-league team, and he quickly set about lighting a fire under the Orioles. Although he could be controversial at times because of his frankness when talking to the media and umpires, Weaver kept his teams in contention year after year and became known as "The Earl of Baltimore."

In 1969, the Orioles were back with a vengeance, storming through the regular season with a club-record 109 victories. The team's offensive power was again provided largely by the Robinsons but was helped considerably by the booming bat of first baseman Boog Powell and the base-path speed of center fielder Paul Blair. Shortstop Mark Belanger and second baseman Davey Johnson provided Gold Glove-winning defense up the middle, and the team's pitching staff also had a fine season, with Mike Cuellar winning 23 games and Palmer chipping in 16.

One of the most popular Orioles ever, Boog Powell was a fun-loving strongman who swatted 339 career homers.

JIM PALMER

Baltimore's longtime ace, Jim Palmer,
won World Series games for the
Orioles in the 1960s, '70s, and '80s.

1970 ORIOLES

After cruising to the AL Eastern Division title (the league was divided into two divisions in 1969), Baltimore swept the Minnesota Twins in three games in the AL Championship Series (ALCS) and advanced to face the New York Mets in the World Series. Featuring stars at nearly every position, the Orioles were heavily favored to beat the "no-name" Mets, who had just barely captured their division. But the "Miracle Mets" proved they were no joke, upsetting Baltimore four games to one to win the World Series.

Stung by the loss, the Orioles came out swinging in 1970. Baltimore went 108–54 to capture the AL East and then defeated Minnesota again in the ALCS to reach the World Series. There the Orioles faced the mighty Cincinnati Reds, who were powered by such legendary stars as Pete Rose, Tony Perez, and Johnny Bench. The Orioles managed to win the first two games at Cincinnati by one run each and then headed back to Baltimore. Brooks Robinson put on a jaw-dropping defensive show and finished the World Series batting .429 with two home runs and six RBI to help the Orioles top the Reds in five games. "Baseball is a team game," said a stunned Earl Weaver, "but what Brooks did is as close as I've ever seen one player come to winning a series by himself."

In 1971, the Orioles' starting pitchers put together a season for the history books. McNally (21), Palmer (20), Cuellar (20), and Pat Dobson (20) became the first pitching staff since the 1920 Chicago White Sox to feature four 20-game winners. The Orioles also received solid contributions from Belanger and outfielders Merv Rettenmund and Don Buford. These players led the Orioles to a third consecutive World Series, this time opposite the Pittsburgh Pirates. The Orioles pushed the series to seven games behind solid pitching performances by Palmer and McNally, but there would be no repeat, as star outfielder Roberto Clemente and the Pirates won the deciding Game 7 by a 2–1 score to claim the championship.

The Orioles continued to fly high through the mid-1970s, capturing division titles in 1973 and 1974 before falling in the playoffs. But by 1978, the team had changed dramatically. Powell and McNally had left the team in 1974, Frank Robinson retired in 1976, and Cuellar and Brooks Robinson were gone by 1977. The old regime had bid farewell, making room for new heroes.

FRANK ROBINSON – Robinson was a reliable power source, averaging almost 30 home runs a season during his Orioles career. After his playing days ended, he became the first black manager in the major leagues (with the Cleveland Indians in 1975).

FRANK ROBINSON

FIRST BASEMAN · EDDIE MURRAY

Eddie Murray spread his wings early as an Orioles star, hitting .283 with 27 home runs and 88 RBI in his first big-league season, earning AL Rookie of the Year honors. He is commonly considered to be the second-greatest switch hitter in major-league history (behind only Yankees legend Mickey Mantle) with career totals of 3,255 hits and 504 home runs. Known for his consistency, he produced at least 75 RBI for a major-league record 20 straight seasons. Although Murray was traded away in 1988, he came back to Baltimore in 1996 and helped the Orioles to their first playoff appearance since 1983 while notching his 500th home run.

EDDIE MURRAY
FIRST BASEMAN

BALTIMORE
ORIOLES

STATS

Orioles seasons: 1977–88, 1996

Height: 6-2

Weight: 200

- **8-time All-Star**
- **3-time Gold Glove winner**
- **19 career grand slams**
- **Baseball Hall of Fame inductee (2003)**

SECOND BASEMAN · DAVEY JOHNSON

A sure-gloved infielder, Johnson developed considerable power at the plate later in his career. He played eight seasons with the Orioles, providing solid defense and a formidable bat in a time when good hitting was considered merely a bonus in second basemen. He teamed with shortstop Mark Belanger to win matching Gold Gloves in the same season twice (in 1969 and 1971). After his playing days, Johnson made a name for himself as a manager for several teams. As the Orioles' skipper, he guided the club to two winning seasons, including trips to the ALCS in 1996 and 1997.

STATS

Orioles seasons: 1965–72

Height: 6-1

Weight: 180

- **4-time All-Star**
- **3-time Gold Glove winner**
- **.981 career fielding percentage**
- **3,862 career putouts**

DAVEY JOHNSON
SECOND BASEMAN

BALTIMORE
ORIOLES

THE TRADE

Throughout professional sports history, the trading of players between teams has been a constant gamble, with some trades leaving obvious winners and losers. On nearly any list of the most lopsided trades in sports history, one will find the Orioles mentioned as the clear winners in a 1965 trade with the Cincinnati Reds. Believing that Frank Robinson's best years were behind him, Reds general manager Bill DeWitt traded the 30-year-old outfielder to the Orioles for pitchers Milt Pappas and Jack Baldschun and outfielder Dick Simpson. It didn't take long for Dewitt to discover his folly. The next season, Robinson won the AL MVP award and the Triple Crown by hitting .316 with 49 home runs and 122 RBI. He went on to play six seasons for the Orioles, helping the team reach the World Series four times. Meanwhile, Pappas posted a career 30–29 record in a Reds uniform, while Baldschun won just 1 game for Cincinnati. Simpson, the third piece of the deal, played only two seasons in a Reds uniform while batting under .260. The deal gave the Orioles some of the best years of a Hall of Fame career, while the Reds received only two seasons of mediocrity.

NEW BIRDS EMERGE

By 1979, a new generation of Orioles stars had stepped to the forefront. Eddie Murray, the 1977 AL Rookie of the Year, was already among the best first basemen in the game. Speedy center fielder Al Bumbry was a base-stealing marvel, and third baseman Doug DeCinces and outfielder Ken Singleton provided abundant power at the plate. The team's pitching staff also was loaded with talented youngsters such as Mike Flanagan and Dennis Martinez.

DOUG DeCINCES – DeCinces was a slow runner but a valuable hitter and sure-handed fielder. The third baseman formed a bridge between two Orioles legends, as he replaced Brooks Robinson in the mid-1970s and was replaced by Cal Ripken Jr. in 1982.

AL BUMBRY

Renowned for his rare speed, Al Bumbry tied the major-league mark for most triples (three) in one game in 1973.

THIRD BASEMAN · BROOKS ROBINSON

Brooks Robinson is widely regarded as the most impressive fielding third baseman in major-league history. More than just a slick fielder, though, Robinson ranks second behind Cal Ripken Jr. in the Baltimore record books for career hits, doubles, and RBI. He helped lead the Orioles to four World Series and was an All-Star for 15 consecutive years. His uniform number (5) was the first to be retired by the Baltimore Orioles at the end of the 1977 season. Cincinnati Reds manager Sparky Anderson once said of the defensive dynamo, "If I dropped this paper plate, he'd pick it up on one hop and throw me out at first."

BROOKS ROBINSON
THIRD BASEMAN

BALTIMORE
ORIOLES

STATS

Orioles seasons: 1955–77

Height: 6-1

Weight: 190

- **1964 AL MVP**

- **16-time Gold Glove winner**

- **2,848 career hits**

- **1970 World Series MVP**

These new Orioles captured the AL East in 1979 with a 102–57 record. After defeating a California Angels team lead by slugging outfielder Don Baylor and strikeout pitcher Nolan Ryan three games to one in the ALCS, Baltimore faced the Pittsburgh Pirates in the World Series once again. The Orioles won three of the series' first five games, but behind star first baseman Willie Stargell and some great Pirates pitching, Pittsburgh won the last two games and the world title.

In 1982, Orioles fans witnessed a passing of the torch from one Baltimore icon to another. Earl Weaver was in his final year as manager when the team called up Cal Ripken Jr., a promising young shortstop. Ripken, whose father was a longtime coach for Baltimore, exploded onto the major-league scene, hitting 28 home runs and driving in 93 runs to capture AL Rookie of the Year honors. The hardworking Ripken also proved durable, not missing a single game after May 29, beginning a streak of consecutive games played that would become his calling card.

In 1983, new manager Joe Altobelli guided the Orioles to a superb season. The team rolled to the AL East title with a 98–64 record, then defeated the Chicago White Sox three games to one to win the pennant. In the World Series, Baltimore lost the opening game to the Philadelphia Phillies. But then the veteran Orioles pitchers took control, surrendering only nine runs for the series as Baltimore won the next four games. Although Murray and catcher Rick Dempsey played well, there was no doubt that it was the men on the mound who won the 1983 World Series for the Orioles. "We have always relied on our pitchers," noted Dempsey. "When you can roll out guys like Palmer, Flanagan, and [Scott] McGregor every day, you're going to win a lot of games."

The Orioles went through a gradual decline during the rest of the 1980s. Although stars such as Murray and Ripken continued to excel, the team's stellar pitching staff began to fall apart. By 1988, Palmer, Flanagan, McGregor, and both Dennis and Tippy Martinez were all gone. Without them, the Orioles suffered a major-league-record 21 straight losses at the start of the 1988 season. As the team limped through the end of the decade, plans for a new ballpark and the return of Frank Robinson as manager kept fans' spirits up as the losses mounted.

The Orioles' sluggish performance continued into the early 1990s. Despite strong performances from Ripken and such newcomers as outfielder Brady Anderson and the pitcher who would become a mainstay in the Baltimore rotation throughout the decade, Mike Mussina, Baltimore continued to hover around the .500 mark. In 1992, the team moved from Memorial Sta-

EDDIE MURRAY – Consistency was the key to "Steady Eddie's" Hall of Fame career. He joined baseball's elite "500 home runs" club despite never hitting more than 33 dingers in a single season. Murray stayed with Baltimore as a coach after retiring as a player.

SHORTSTOP · CAL RIPKEN JR.

The ultimate "Iron Man," Ripken played in a record 2,632 consecutive games in the major leagues, every one in a Baltimore Orioles uniform. Originally called to the major leagues as a promising young third baseman, Ripken split time between third and shortstop. He wasted no time in making a name for himself, hitting a home run in his very first at bat, winning AL Rookie of the Year honors in 1982, and capturing the AL MVP award the next season. During Ripken's 21-year career with Baltimore, the soft-spoken shortstop was the heart of the team, leading by his hardworking example rather than words.

STATS

Orioles seasons: 1981–2001

Height: 6-4

Weight: 225

- **2-time AL MVP**

- **19-time All-Star**

- **2-time Gold Glove winner**

- **431 career HR**

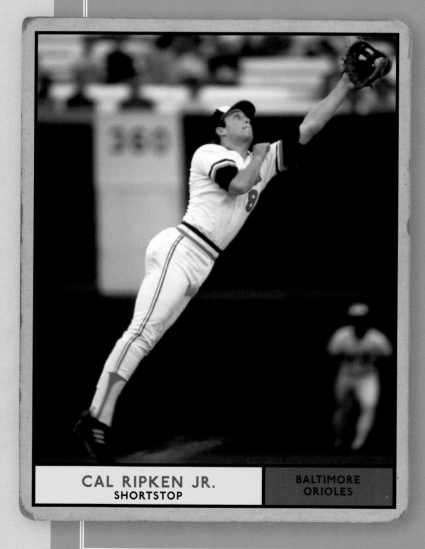

CAL RIPKEN JR.
SHORTSTOP

BALTIMORE
ORIOLES

dium into its new, baseball-only facility, Oriole Park at Camden Yards. A scenic ballfield, Camden Yards was a simple yet stunning throwback to the earlier days of baseball that was embraced by fans and soon mimicked by other franchises around the league. Seemingly inspired by the new facility, the Orioles responded with two straight winning seasons.

In 1994, the Orioles added slugging first baseman Rafael Palmeiro to the roster and were in a division title chase until a players' strike ended the season in August. The following year, the team took a step backward with a third-place finish in the AL East, though the fans were treated to a special night on September 6 as Ripken surpassed Lou "Iron Horse" Gehrig's consecutive game mark by playing in his 2,131st game. Ripken's streak would continue until September 20, 1998, when he would ask out of the lineup for the first time in 16 years. The streak of 2,632 consecutive games played stands as one of baseball's most impressive records—one that may never be broken.

Driven by the great play of Ripken, Palmeiro, Anderson, and sure-handed second baseman Roberto Alomar, the Orioles returned to prominence in 1996 and 1997, winning their division and reaching the ALCS both years. The Yankees bounced the Orioles in the 1996 ALCS, four games to one, on their way to winning the World Series. In 1997, it was a Cleveland Indians team sparked by slugging first baseman Jim Thome that stopped the Orioles four games to two, despite excellent Baltimore pitching.

MIKE CUELLAR

BIRDS ON THE HILL

The Orioles can lay claim to what might be the most dominant back-to-back pitching seasons in major-league history. In 1970, the staff was led by former Cy Young Award winner Mike Cuellar, who earned 24 wins with his devastating "palm-ball" pitch. Lefty Dave McNally also won 24 games, and the youngest hurler of the bunch, flamethrower Jim Palmer, added 20 along with a team-high 199 strikeouts. Together, the threesome accounted for 68 of the Orioles' 108 victories during the 1970 season. Baltimore's Birds, however, were just getting warmed up. The next year, they had not three, but four starters eclipse the prestigious 20-win mark. Cuellar again had a spectacular season, winning 20 games. Palmer also won 20 contests while tallying 184 strikeouts. McNally topped each of them with 21 victories and only 5 losses. But what made 1971 even better than 1970 was Pat Dobson. A curveball pitcher acquired from the San Diego Padres, Dobson also hurled his way to 20 victories. This phenomenal pitching propelled the Orioles to the 1971 World Series. The Orioles lost the series in seven games to the Pittsburgh Pirates, but their pitching could hardly be faulted; the Pirates didn't score more than five runs in any game.

LEFT FIELDER · JOHN LOWENSTEIN

On every great team, there are the big stars, and then there are those players who simply help the team win. John Lowenstein was one of the latter. When the game was on the line, Lowenstein was at his best. In 1979, he provided a pinch-hit home run in Game 1 of the ALCS and a pinch two-run double in Game 4 of the World Series. He furthered his reputation as a clutch hitter in 1983 when he slammed a game-tying home run in the eighth inning of Game 2 of the World Series to help the Orioles win it all.

STATS

Orioles seasons: 1979–85

Height: 6-0

Weight: 175

- **128 career stolen bases**
- **116 career HR**
- **.984 career fielding percentage**
- **.385 BA in 1983 World Series**

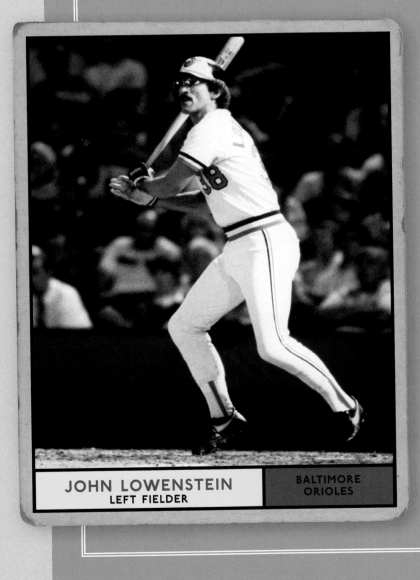

JOHN LOWENSTEIN
LEFT FIELDER

BALTIMORE ORIOLES

MIGUEL TEJADA

Miguel Tejada led the Orioles into the new millennium, making the All-Star Game in 2004, 2005, and 2006.

STRUGGLING FOR FLIGHT

fter 1997, the Orioles' fortunes declined. The organization had gotten away from its formula of developing its own players through its minor-league system and had gotten into the expensive habit of signing free agents—such as outfielder Eric Davis and designated hitter Joe Carter in 1998 and outfielder Albert Belle in 1999—to shore up weak areas. This strategy of signing veterans in the late stages of their careers left the team with a huge payroll and few young impact players.

Individual milestones continued to pile up for Ripken as he reached 400 home runs in 1999 and 3,000 hits in 2000, making him one of only seven major-leaguers ever to reach both marks. At the beginning of the 2001 season, Ripken announced that his 21st season would be his last. "Cal's retirement brings an end to one of the finest, most noble careers this game has ever seen," said Orioles Hall-of-Famer Brooks Robinson.

From 2000 to 2003, the Orioles posted losing records every season, finishing fourth in the tough AL East every year. Right fielder Jay Gibbons opened eyes by slugging 28 home runs in 2002, but Ripken was gone, longtime standout hurler Mike Mussina had jumped ship for a richer contract with the Yan-

A FAMILY AFFAIR

When one thinks about famous baseball families, certain names spring to mind. There were great father-son combos such as Bobby and Barry Bonds and Ken Griffey Sr. and Jr. One family, the Boones, managed to put three generations in the big leagues. But the Baltimore Orioles can pride themselves on being the only team ever to feature two brothers who were managed by their father at the major-league level. From 1988 to 1992, the Orioles' double-play combo consisted of Cal Ripken Jr. at shortstop and his younger brother Bill at second base. The brothers were officially on the roster together for the first time in 1987, although they did not become the starting middle infield duo until the next season. Cal Ripken Sr. managed the team for the entirety of the 1987 season but was fired only six games into the 1988 campaign. Cal Sr. spent 36 years in the Baltimore organization as a minor-league player, scout, coach, and manager. Cal Jr. enjoyed a 21-year career with the major-league club, and Bill spent a total of seven seasons wearing an Orioles uniform. Perhaps no family has contributed as much to a major-league franchise as the Ripkens have to the Orioles.

CENTER FIELDER · BRADY ANDERSON

Sometimes called the most unlikely 50-home run hitter in baseball history, Brady Anderson turned heads in 1996. Never before or after did he top 24 home runs in a year, but during that 1996 season, his bat was on fire. He put up a .297 average with 50 home runs and 110 RBI, surpassing Frank Robinson as the Orioles' record-holder for home runs in a season. Anderson was more than just a one-year power surge, however; his speed made him a fine center fielder and helped him steal a club-record 307 bases in his career.

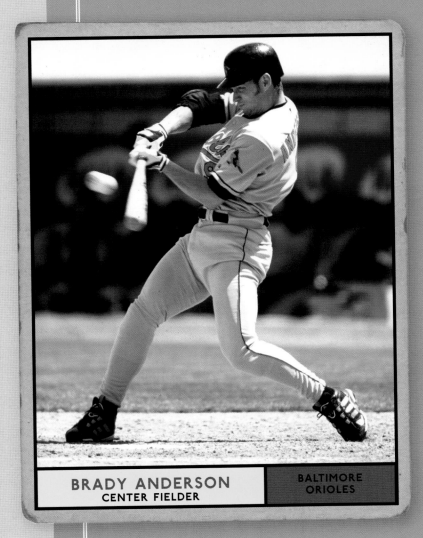

BRADY ANDERSON
CENTER FIELDER

BALTIMORE
ORIOLES

STATS

Orioles seasons: 1988–2001

Height: 6-1

Weight: 185

- **3-time All-Star**

- **.989 career fielding percentage**

- **1,062 career runs scored**

- **3-time AL leader in times hit by pitch**

RIGHT FIELDER · **PAUL BLAIR**

A spectacular defensive outfielder, Paul Blair was known for his ability to get back on the deepest fly balls, a skill that allowed him to play a shallow outfield and take away many base hits. His best year at the plate was 1969, when he hit for a .285 average, 26 home runs, and 76 RBI. But his consistency and speed put him in the top five in club history in doubles, triples, and steals. Blair was a crucial part of the Orioles' World Series teams of the 1960s and '70s, making several spectacular catches in key playoff games.

STATS

Orioles seasons: 1964–76

Height: 6-0

Weight: 171

- **2-time All-Star**

- **8-time Gold Glove winner**

- **171 career stolen bases**

- **282 career doubles**

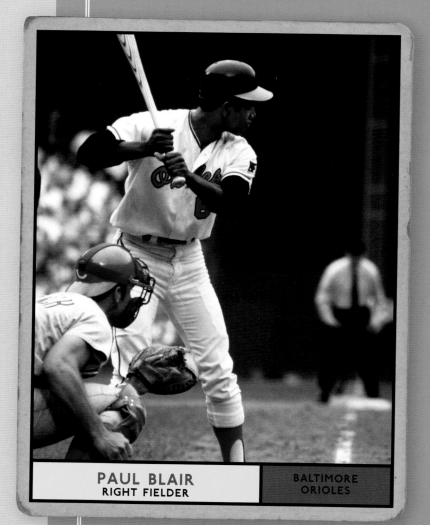

PAUL BLAIR
RIGHT FIELDER

BALTIMORE
ORIOLES

kees, and third baseman and RBI machine Tony Batista left town as a free agent at the end of 2003. It was rebuilding time in Baltimore.

In 2004, the team made two notable acquisitions in slugging catcher Javy Lopez and shortstop Miguel Tejada, the 2002 AL MVP. The signings paid dividends immediately. Lopez hit .316 in 2004, bashing 23 home runs and driving in 86 runs. Meanwhile, Tejada, an outstanding all-around player who seemed to hit best with players in scoring position, set a new team record

BRIAN ROBERTS – The second baseman joined the big leagues in 2001 and slowly rose to star status in Baltimore. He showed a strong bat in 2004 by hitting an AL-best 50 doubles, then revealed his speed on the base paths by stealing 36 bases in 2006.

AN ALL-STAR WELCOME

Upon its official opening at the beginning of the 1992 season, Oriole Park at Camden Yards—a venue built with brick walls—was considered one of the most beautiful and fan-friendly ballparks in all of baseball. As a tip of the hat to the new ballpark, Major League Baseball elected to make Camden Yards home to the 1993 All-Star Game, an event that provided two of the most memorable moments in All-Star history. During the Home Run Derby, some of the game's top sluggers competed to see who could "go yard" most often. Although Texas Rangers outfielder Juan Gonzalez won the competition, it was Seattle Mariners outfielder Ken Griffey Jr. who stole the show by becoming the first player ever to hit the B&O Warehouse building that stands 439 feet away from home plate. The next night, during the All-Star Game, Philadelphia Phillies first baseman John Kruk provided one of the most comical at bats in the history of the "Midsummer Classic." After intimidating Seattle Mariners pitcher Randy Johnson whistled a blazing fastball behind Kruk's head, the husky Kruk moved to the outside of the batter's box and flailed wildly for the rest of the at bat in exaggerated fear of Johnson's heater.

with an AL-high 150 RBI. Such feats convinced Orioles manager Lee Mazzilli that the Baltimore lineup was ready to compete for the division again. "This is a good, good ballclub," he said. "This is a club that can compete with any team in the league. That's what I believe."

Hoping to add one more big stick to the lineup, the Orioles traded for disgruntled Chicago Cubs slugger Sammy Sosa in 2005. But unlike Tejada and Lopez, Sosa didn't bring his best form when he donned Baltimore orange and black. The once-feared slugger hit just .221 with 14 home runs before retiring after the season. Distracted by off-field controversies—such as steroid allegations against longtime first baseman Rafael Palmeiro—and slowed by injuries to key players, the team finished 74–88 in 2005.

Heading into the 2006 season, the Orioles extended the contract of manager Sam Perlozzo, who had taken over for Mazzilli in August 2005. Formerly a bench coach for the team, Perlozzo was a firm believer in the Oriole Way—playing with maximum effort game after game and focusing on the fundamentals. "We're going to go at it as hard as we can, and as long as we can, until we get a winner on this field," he announced to fans. "I look for that to happen sooner than later."

A winning season seemed within reach in 2006 as Perlozzo relied on the

"O!" WHAT FANS!

From the time that the St. Louis Browns moved to Baltimore and became the Orioles, fan support for the team has been tremendous. It didn't take long for certain traditions to develop, either. Since the 1970s, it has been a custom at Orioles home games for fans to vocally accent the "Oh!" in the opening line of "The Star Spangled Banner." To this day, fans at Camden Yards carry on this practice, even though some people have viewed it as disrespectful to the national anthem. The excitement over the "O" vowel sound comes twofold, from the first letter in the word "Orioles," to the most distinguishable sound in the Baltimorean accent.

Orioles fans don't stop at "The Star Spangled Banner," though. During the seventh-inning stretch, the Camden Yards speakers play country singer John Denver's "Thank God I'm a Country Boy," and the crowd enthusiastically holds an "Oooohh!" as Denver draws out a long note during the bridge. The tradition also includes the chant of "Oh-wee-oh, we-oh-oh" from The Wizard of Oz and the song "Oh Yeah!" by the 1980s pop group Yellow. These vocal traditions make for an enthusiastic and entertaining experience at Camden Yards, whether the Orioles are winning or not.

MANAGER · EARL WEAVER

A colorful character with vast baseball knowledge, Weaver won 1,480 games as a big-league manager, putting him 20th on the all-time wins list. He managed 18 seasons—all for the Orioles. Weaver led the team to the World Series four different times, coming away with a world championship in 1970. Never a fan of "small ball," Weaver liked to have powerful hitters in his lineup and pitchers who could hold the other team down. Weaver is perhaps remembered most for his fiery demeanor; he set a major-league record by being ejected from 98 games, including both ends of a double-header in 1985.

STATS

Orioles seasons as manager: 1968–82, 1985–86

Height: 5-7

Weight: 175

Managerial Record: 1,480–1,060

World Series Championship: 1970

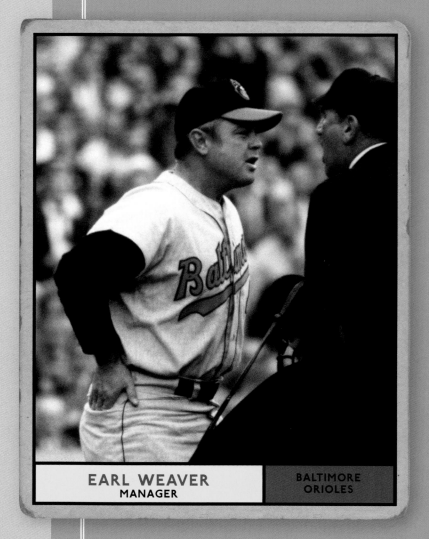

EARL WEAVER
MANAGER

BALTIMORE
ORIOLES

formidable nucleus of Tejada, Lopez, and second baseman Brian Roberts. Orioles fans also cheered the efforts of a pitching rotation that featured veteran Kris Benson and talented young starter Erik Bedard. Baltimore played .500 ball the first two months of the season in the highly competitive AL East before sliding down the standings. Tejada was again an offensive powerhouse, but the club ended the year 70–92. Still, Perlozzo believed the Orioles were headed for better days. "This year, we'll try to be a little more demanding of our ballclub all the way around," the manager said as Baltimore prepared to start spring training in 2007. "I think we're on the verge of getting to the next level, so I think we have to be serious about it and go after it."

With a history that includes seven World Series appearances and three world championships—not to mention a slew of stars with such names as Robinson, Palmer, and Ripken—the Baltimore Orioles have built an enviable tradition. Even in the club's down seasons, fans have found heroes to put hope in and feats worth cheering for. As today's Orioles take on the AL's best in beautiful Camden Yards, orange and black may soon become the colors of champions once again.